To

From

Date

Every house where love abides and friendship
is a guest, is surely home, and home, sweet
home; for there the heart can rest.

HENRY VAN DYKE

Post Card

ADDRESS ONLY

Friends Rule the Roost

Artwork by
Susan Winget

HARVEST HOUSE PUBLISHERS
EUGENE, OREGON

Friends Rule the Roost

Text copyright © 2014 by Harvest House Publishers
Artwork copyright © by Susan Winget

Published by Harvest House Publishers
Eugene, Oregon 97402
www.harvesthousepublishers.com

ISBN 978-0-7369-6224-7

The artwork of Susan Winget is used by Harvest House Publishers, Inc. under authorization from Courtney Davis, Inc. For more information regarding art prints featured in this book, please contact:

Courtney Davis, Inc.
55 Francisco Street, Suite 450
San Francisco, CA 94133
www.susanwinget.com

Design and production by Garborg Design Works, Savage, Minnesota

Harvest House Publishers has made every effort to trace the ownership of all poems and quotes. In the event of a question arising from the use of a poem or quote, we regret any error made and will be pleased to make the necessary correction in future editions of this book.

All Scripture verses are taken from the Holy Bible, New International Version®, NIV®. Copyright © 1973, 1978, 1984, 2011 by Biblica, Inc.® Used by permission. All rights reserved worldwide.

Printed in China

14 15 16 17 18 19 20 21 /FC / 10 9 8 7 6 5 4 3 2 1

Delicious Recipes and Fun Do-It-Yourself Projects

Life is made up, not of great sacrifices or duties, but of little things in which smiles, and kindnesses, and small obligations, given habitually, are what win and preserve the heart and secure comfort.

SIR HUMPHRY DAVY

IN THE COOKIES OF LIFE, FRIENDS ARE THE CHOCOLATE CHIPS.

AUTHOR UNKNOWN

Stay is a charming word in a friend's vocabulary.

AMOS BRONSON ALCOTT

OUR FRIENDSHIP IS

A true friend... advises justly, assists readily, adventures boldly, takes all patiently, defends courageously, and continues a friend unchangeably.

WILLIAM PENN

The true source of cheerfulness is benevolence. The soul that perpetually overflows with kindness and sympathy will always be cheerful.

P. GODWIN

Friends...they cherish each other's hopes. They are kind to each other's dreams.

HENRY DAVID THOREAU

EGGS-ACTLY RIGHT!

Honey Cornbread Muffins

1 cup yellow cornmeal
1 cup all-purpose flour
1 tablespoon baking powder
½ cup granulated sugar
1 teaspoon salt
1 cup whole milk
2 large eggs
¼ cup butter, melted
¼ cup honey

Combine cornmeal, flour, baking powder, sugar, and salt in a large mixing bowl. In another bowl, whisk together the milk, eggs, butter, and honey. Add the wet to the dry ingredients and stir until just mixed. Pour the cornbread mixture evenly into 12 paper-lined muffin cups. Bake in a preheated 400° oven for 15 minutes.

The better part of one's life consists of his friendships.

ABRAHAM LINCOLN

Easy Morning Glory Muffins

2 cups all-purpose flour
1¼ cups granulated sugar
2 teaspoons baking soda
2 teaspoons ground cinnamon
¼ teaspoon salt
2 cups shredded carrots
½ cup raisins
½ cup chopped walnuts
½ cup unsweetened flaked coconut
1 apple (peeled, cored, and shredded)
3 eggs
1 cup vegetable oil
2 teaspoons vanilla extract

Mix flour, sugar, baking soda, cinnamon, and salt together in a large mixing bowl. Stir in the carrots, raisins, nuts, coconut, and apple. In another bowl, beat together the eggs, oil, and vanilla. Stir the egg mixture into the flour mixture just until moistened. Scoop batter evenly into 12 paper-lined muffin cups. Bake in a preheated 350° oven for 20 minutes or until a toothpick inserted into the center of a muffin comes out clean.

HOW TO MAKE CANDLES

Materials

+ candle mold (tins, jars, teacups, or other containers that can withstand heat)
+ wax (paraffin, soy, beeswax, or partially used candles)
+ essential oils (can be purchased at a craft store) for scent
+ oil-based dye (can be purchased at a craft store) for color
+ wick
+ tape, scissors, pencils

1. Cover the work area with newspaper.

2. Prepare the wax by cutting or shredding it into chunks or shavings.

3. Melt the wax slowly using a double boiler.

4. If desired add scent to the melted wax and stir well.

5. Add color to the melted wax and stir well.

6. Place a wick in the center of a candle mold. To do this, tape the bottom of the wick to the center bottom of the mold. Loop the top of the wick around the middle of a pencil and rest the pencil across the top of the mold. Make sure the wick is straight up and down.

7. Slowly pour the melted wax into the mold. Allow to cool 24 hours.

8. Trim the wick to 1/4 inch from the top of the candle.

LOVE SOUGHT IS GOOD, BUT
GIV'N UNSOUGHT IS BETTER.

WILLIAM SHAKESPEARE

That day is lost on which
one has not laughed.

FRENCH PROVERB

One who has unreliable friends soon comes to ruin,
but there is a friend who sticks closer than a brother.

THE BOOK OF PROVERBS

Who can wonder I love to stay,
Week after week, here hidden away,
In this sly nook that I love the best—
This little brown house like a ground-bird's nest?

ELLA WHEELER WILCOX

YOU'RE ONE GOOD EGG!

A laugh, to be joyous,
must flow from a
joyous heart, for
without kindness, there
can be no true joy.

THOMAS CARLYLE

All God's pleasures are simple
ones; the rapture of a May
morning sunshine, the stream blue
and green, kind words, benevolent
acts, the glow of good humor.

FREDERICK WILLIAM ROBERTSON

Banana Crumb Muffins

1½ cups all-purpose flour
1 teaspoon baking soda
1 teaspoon baking powder
½ teaspoon salt
3 bananas (mashed)
¾ cup granulated sugar
1 egg (lightly beaten)
⅓ cup butter (melted)
⅓ cup packed brown sugar
2 tablespoons all-purpose flour
⅛ teaspoon ground cinnamon
1 tablespoon butter

Mix 1½ cups flour, baking soda, baking powder, and salt together in a large mixing bowl. In another bowl, beat together bananas, sugar, egg, and melted butter. Stir the banana mixture into the flour mixture just until moistened. Spoon batter evenly into 12 paper-lined muffin cups. In a small bowl, mix together brown sugar, 2 tablespoons flour, and cinnamon. Cut in 1 tablespoon butter until mixture resembles coarse cornmeal. Sprinkle over muffins. Bake in a preheated 375° oven for 18 to 20 minutes or until a toothpick inserted into the center of a muffin comes out clean.

I had rather be on my farm than be emperor of the world.

GEORGE WASHINGTON

Hot Spiced Tea

6 cups water
1 teaspoon whole cloves
1 (1-inch) piece of cinnamon stick
6 tea bags black tea
¾ cup orange juice
½ cup granulated sugar
¼ cup pineapple juice
2 tablespoons lemon juice

Pour water into a kettle and add cloves and cinnamon. Bring to a boil. Remove from heat, add tea bags, and steep for 5 minutes. Remove cloves, cinnamon, and tea bags and set aside. In a saucepan, bring orange juice, sugar, pineapple juice, and lemon juice to a boil, stirring constantly until sugar is completely dissolved. Remove from heat and pour into the spiced tea. Serve hot. Makes 6 servings.

How to Make a Quilted Table Runner

Materials

+ fabric remnants for strips
+ fabric for back and binding
+ batting
+ scissors, safety pins, thread

1. Cut 25 (2½" x 10½") strips of fabric.

2. Arrange fabric strips in sets of five, paying attention to how the fabric colors and patterns coordinate with each other.

3. Sew 5 strips together along the long edge with a scant ¼" seam allowance. Press seams open. Repeat 5 more times to make 5 quilt blocks.

4. Sew the blocks together, alternating the strip direction each time. Press seams open.

5. Layer the backing, batting, and runner top. Smooth out all the wrinkles and pin with safety pins.

6. Machine quilt runner ¼" from each seam.

7. Trim the batting and backing from around entire runner.

8. Sew binding on.

One should take good care not to grow too wise for so great a pleasure of life as laughter.

JOSEPH ADDISON

There are souls in this world who have the gift of finding joy everywhere, and leaving it behind them when they go.

FREDERICK WILLIAM FABER

A true friend is a forever friend.

GEORGE MacDONALD

I'M CROWING ABOUT YOU!

Love is all very well in its way,
but friendship is much higher.
Indeed, I know of nothing in
the world that is either nobler or
rarer than a devoted friendship.

OSCAR WILDE

Honesty is the
first chapter in the
book of wisdom.

THOMAS JEFFERSON

TWO ARE BETTER THAN ONE,
BECAUSE THEY HAVE A GOOD
RETURN FOR THEIR LABOR:
IF EITHER OF THEM FALLS DOWN,
ONE CAN HELP THE OTHER UP.

THE BOOK OF ECCLESIASTES

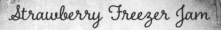

Strawberry Freezer Jam

2 cups crushed fresh strawberries
4 cups granulated sugar
1 (1.75 ounce) package dry pectin
¾ cup water

Mix crushed strawberries with sugar and let stand for 10 minutes. In a small saucepan, stir the pectin into the water. Bring to a boil over medium-high heat and boil for 1 minute while stirring constantly. Stir the boiling water into the strawberry mixture and continue to vigorously stir for at least 3 minutes. Let stand for another 3 minutes before pouring jam into jars or other storage containers. Wipe off top edges of containers and immediately cover with lids. Allow to cool and then store in freezer for up to 1 year or in the refrigerator up to 3 weeks. Makes 5 pints.

A joy shared is a joy doubled.

JOHANN WOLFGANG VON GOETHE

All-Day Apple Butter

5½ pounds apples (peeled, cored, and finely chopped)
4 cups granulated sugar
2 teaspoons ground cinnamon
¼ teaspoon ground cloves
¼ teaspoon salt

Place apples in a slow cooker. In a medium bowl, mix the sugar, cinnamon, cloves, and salt. Pour the mixture over the apples and mix well. Cover and cook on high 1 hour. Reduce heat to low and cook 9 to 11 hours, stirring occasionally, until the mixture is thickened and dark brown. Uncover and continue cooking on low 1 hour. Spoon the mixture into sterile containers and cover. Store in the refrigerator for up to 2 weeks or freeze for up to 2 months. Makes 4 pints.

How to Make a Milk-Jug Bird Feeder

Materials

+ clean empty milk jug
+ marker
+ thin wire or strong string
+ scissors
+ birdseed

1. Using the marker, outline holes (about 2½ inches in diameter) on the 2 sides of the milk jug away from the handle. Cut out.

2. Remove the lid, wrap wire or string around the base of the opening, and replace the lid. The wire will be used to hang the feeder from a tree branch.

3. With scissors, poke holes in the bottom of the jug for drainage.

4. Fill the Milk-Jug Bird Feeder with birdseed and hang it outside near a window.

I do not wish to treat friendships daintily, but with the roughest courage. When they are real, they are not glass threads or frost-work, but the solidest thing we know.

HENRY DAVID THOREAU

Blessed is the influence of one true, loving human soul on another.

GEORGE ELIOT

YES, WE MUST EVER BE FRIENDS; AND OF ALL WHO OFFER YOU FRIENDSHIP
LET ME BE EVER THE FIRST, THE TRUEST, THE NEAREST AND DEAREST!

HENRY WADSWORTH LONGFELLOW

TOGETHER WE

THERE IS ONLY
ONE HAPPINESS IN
THIS LIFE, TO LOVE
AND BE LOVED.

GEORGE SAND

I want a warm and faithful friend,
To cheer the adverse hour;
Who ne'er to flatter will descend,
Nor bend the knee to power.
A friend to chide me when I'm wrong,
My inmost soul to see;
And that my friendship prove as strong
To him as his to me.

JOHN QUINCY ADAMS

RULE THE ROOST.

Pecan Coffee Cake

2 cups all-purpose flour
1/4 teaspoon salt
1 tablespoon baking powder
1 cup butter (softened)
1 cup sour cream
1½ cups granulated sugar
2 eggs
1 tablespoon vanilla extract

Topping
½ cup brown sugar
1 cup chopped pecans
1 teaspoon ground cinnamon
2 tablespoons butter (melted)

Sift flour, salt, and baking powder together into a medium bowl and set aside. In a large mixing bowl, cream the butter until light and fluffy. Gradually beat in sour cream and then the sugar. Beat in eggs one at a time. Stir in vanilla. By hand, fold in the flour mixture, mixing just until moistened. Spread batter into a 9x13-inch pan lined with aluminum foil that has been lightly greased. Combine all topping ingredients in a small bowl, mix well, and spread evenly over the cake. Bake in a preheated 350° oven for 30 to 35 minutes or until a toothpick inserted into the center comes out clean. Let cool in pan for 10 minutes, and then turn out onto a wire rack and remove foil.

Cinnamon Crumb Coffee Cake

2 cups all-purpose flour
1 cup plus 2 tablespoons granulated sugar
1 teaspoon salt
10 tablespoons unsalted butter
(lightly softened)
1 teaspoon baking powder
½ teaspoon baking soda
¾ cup buttermilk (at room temperature)
1 large egg
2 teaspoons vanilla extract
⅔ cup brown sugar
2 teaspoons ground cinnamon

Mix the flour, sugar, and salt together in a large mixing bowl. Cut in butter until the mixture resembles coarse crumbs. Set aside 1 cup of the mixture. Mix the baking powder and baking soda into the remaining flour mixture. Beat in buttermilk, egg, and vanilla until the batter is smooth and fluffy. Spoon the batter into a generously greased 9-inch springform pan (or 9 x 9 x 2-inch baking pan). Add the brown sugar and cinnamon to the reserved flour mixture. Mix well. Sprinkle over the batter, pressing lightly so it sticks. Bake in a preheated 350° oven for 50 to 55 minutes or until a toothpick inserted into the center comes out clean. Allow to cool 10 minutes. Remove the sides of the springform pan and allow cake to cool completely before serving.

My command is this: Love each other as I have loved you.
THE BOOK OF JOHN

How to Make Moisturizing Lotion

Ingredients

- ✦ ½ cup oil (grape seed oil for sensitive skin, almond oil for normal skin)
- ✦ 2 tablespoons emulsifier (beeswax or petroleum jelly)
- ✦ 2 to 3 tablespoons distilled water

1. Combine oil and emulsifier in a microwave-safe glass bowl.

2. Heat the mixture on the medium temperature setting, checking every 30 seconds until the ingredients have completely melted.

3. Slowly pour distilled water into the mixture, stirring briskly with a whisk until everything is blended. For a fluffier lotion, use a stick blender.

4. Allow to cool. Spoon into a clean jar and enjoy.

Extras

If desired, add the following ingredients to personalize the lotion.
- · Vitamin E taken from a supplement capsule preserves the life of the blend and adds more moisturizing power.
- · Rose water (2 drops per 1 cup of lotion) softens skin and relieves inflammation.
- · Essential oils (a total of 2 drops per 1 cup of lotion) of pot marigold (calendula), yarrow, and lavender—used separately or combined—promote healthy skin and smell lovely.

Friendship is a strong and habitual inclination in two persons to promote the good and happiness in one another.

EUSTACE BUDGELL

BIRDS OF A FEATHER

But the mind never unbends itself so agreeably as in the conversation of a well-chosen friend. There is indeed no blessing of life that is any way comparable to the enjoyment of a discreet and virtuous friend. It eases and unloads the mind, clears and improves the understanding, engenders thoughts and knowledge, animates virtue and good resolutions, soothes and allays the passions, and finds employment for most of the vacant hours of life.

JOSEPH ADDISON

Blessed are they who have the gift of making friends, for it is one of God's best gifts. It involves many things, but above all, the power of going out of one's self, and appreciating whatever is noble and loving in another.

THOMAS HUGHES

$\mathcal{A}$ true friend is the gift of God, and he only who made hearts can unite them.

ROBERT SMITH

FLOCK TOGETHER.

$\mathcal{E}$VERY ONE MUST HAVE FELT THAT A CHEERFUL FRIEND IS LIKE A SUNNY DAY, WHICH SHEDS ITS BRIGHTNESS ON ALL AROUND.

SIR JOHN LUBBOCK

$\mathcal{W}$ho finds a faithful friend, finds a treasure.

JEWISH PROVERB

Homemade Hot Cocoa Mix

3 cups nonfat dry milk
2 cups powdered sugar
1½ cups cocoa powder
1½ cups white chocolate chips
¼ teaspoon salt

In a large bowl, mix all ingredients.
Place half the mixture in a food
processor and pulse until the white
chocolate is finely ground. Do the
same with the remaining half. Store in
an airtight container up to 3 months.
To make hot cocoa, stir ⅓ cup cocoa
mix into 1 cup hot milk. Top with
whipped cream or marshmallows.
Makes 20 servings.

By friendship you mean the greatest love, the greatest usefulness, the most open communication, the noblest sufferings, the severest truth, the heartiest counsel, and the greatest union of minds of which brave men and women are capable.

JEREMY TAYLOR

Featherlight Scones

3 cups all-purpose flour
3 teaspoons baking powder
½ teaspoon baking soda
½ teaspoon salt
1 cup cold butter (cubed)
1 egg
1 cup vanilla yogurt
½ teaspoon vanilla extract
2 teaspoons milk
sugar

In a large mixing bowl, stir together the flour, baking powder, baking soda, and salt. Cut in the butter until coarse crumbs form. Stir in egg, yogurt, and vanilla just until combined. Knead dough on lightly floured surface 6 to 8 times. Pat dough into a 9-inch circle and cut into 8 wedges. Place on a lightly greased baking sheet, brush tops with milk, sprinkle with sugar, and bake in a preheated 425° oven for 12 to 15 minutes or until golden brown. Makes 8 scones.

How to Make a Coffee Bean Candle Holder

Materials

+ small votive candle holders
+ whole coffee beans
+ tea lights

Fill small, inexpensive glass or ceramic candle holders with whole coffee beans. Place tea light candles in the center of each candle holder. Light and enjoy the aroma of fresh brewed coffee.

FRIENDS FOREVER

To think that her friend
loved her in return brought a
sensation of deep happiness,
not unmixed with gratitude.
Dinah Maria Mulock

34

A friend loves at all times, and a brother is born for a time of adversity.

THE BOOK OF PROVERBS

I'm so glad that you're my friend. I know our friendship will never end.

ROBERT ALAN

HOLD A TRUE FRIEND WITH BOTH YOUR HANDS.

NIGERIAN PROVERB

AND EVER!

The most I can do for my friend is simply to be his friend. I have no wealth to bestow on him. If he knows that I am happy in loving him, he will want no other reward. Is not friendship divine in this?

HENRY DAVID THOREAU

FRIENDS ARE
THE SUNSHINE
OF LIFE.

JOHN HAY

Cranberry Eggnog Cornbread Scones

2 cups all-purpose flour
½ cup cornmeal
⅓ cup granulated sugar
1 tablespoon baking powder
½ teaspoon salt
⅓ cup butter, chilled
¾ cup sweetened, dried cranberries
⅔ cup eggnog

In a large mixing bowl, stir together the flour, cornmeal, sugar, baking powder, and salt. Cut in the butter until coarse crumbs form. Stir in the cranberries. Use a fork to mix in the eggnog to make a sticky dough. Turn the dough out onto a lightly floured surface and knead dough about 10 times. Pat dough out to ½-inch thick and use a 2-inch diameter biscuit cutter to cut out 8 to 10 rounds. Bake on a lightly greased baking sheet in a preheated 375° oven for about 15 minutes or until golden brown. Makes 8 scones.

Birdseed Treats

²/₃ cup sesame seeds
¹/₃ cup sunflower seeds
¹/₃ cup honey
¹/₃ cup natural, creamy peanut butter
¹/₄ cup flax seeds

Toast the sesame and sunflower seeds in a dry, heavy skillet over medium heat until light brown. Heat honey and peanut butter in a saucepan over low heat until warm. Stir in toasted seeds and flax seeds. Press the mixture into a 9 x 9-inch square pan that's been lined with plastic wrap. After the mixture has cooled completely, cut into bars. Makes 16 bars.

Life is so short, and friendship so precious!

Julia Ward Howe

QUALITY FEED

How to Make an Angels-in-a-Jar Night Lantern

Materials

+ clear glass jar with lid
+ 3 glow sticks (any color)
+ glitter (any size, any color)
+ rubber gloves
+ scissors

1. While wearing the rubber gloves, hold one glow stick at a time over the open jar, snip off one end, and carefully pour all the contents into the jar.

2. Add glitter to the jar.

3. Seal the jar tightly with the lid.

4. To make the "angels" appear, shake the jar so the glow stick material coats the inside of the jar. Note that the light from the glow sticks last 2 to 3 hours. When the glow grows dim, add contents from more glow sticks.

Extras

Turn the jar upside down for a lantern effect. Add tulle to the jar before pouring in the glow stick material to diffuse the effect.

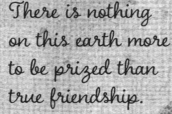

There is nothing on this earth more to be prized than true friendship.

SAINT THOMAS AQUINAS

There is no friend like an old friend who has shared our morning days, no greeting like his welcome, no homage like his praise.

OLIVER WENDELL HOLMES

I AM BLESSED TO

Are we not like two volumes of one book?

MARCELINE DESBORDES-VALMORE

ONE OF THE MOST BEAUTIFUL QUALITIES OF TRUE FRIENDSHIP IS TO UNDERSTAND AND TO BE UNDERSTOOD.

Lucius Annaeus Seneca

The glory of friendship is not the outstretched hand, nor the kindly smile, nor the joy of companionship; it is the spiritual inspiration that comes to one when he discovers that someone else believes in him and is willing to trust him with his friendship. My friends have come unsought. The great God gave them to me.

Ralph Waldo Emerson

CALL YOU FRIEND.

eele Creek, NC

100 lbs. Net W

You are my loyal, loving, lifelong friend.

NOTHING BUT HEAVEN ITSELF
IS BETTER THAN A FRIEND
WHO IS REALLY A FRIEND.

PLAUTUS

Nesting Chicks

1 (10½-ounce) package miniature
marshmallows
2 tablespoons butter
1 teaspoon water
4 drops green food coloring
1½ cups flaked coconut
6 cups Corn Pops
½ cup jelly beans
16 peeps

In a large pan, heat and stir
marshmallows and butter over low
heat until melted and smooth. In a
small plastic bag, combine water and
food coloring and then add the coconut.
Shake to tint and then set aside. Place
the cereal in a large mixing bowl. Add
the marshmallow mixture and stir until
well blended. Press cereal mixture into
16 greased muffin cups. When ready to
serve, remove the cooled nests, layer on
tinted coconut and jelly beans, and top
each with a Peep. Makes 16 nests.

Farm Macaroons

4 egg whites
1/2 teaspoon vanilla extract
1/4 teaspoon almond extract
1/8 teaspoon cream of tartar
1 1/4 cups granulated sugar
1/4 cup all-purpose flour
1/4 teaspoon salt
2 1/2 cups flaked coconut

In a medium mixing bowl, beat egg whites, vanilla extract, almond extract, and cream of tartar until soft peaks form. Gradually beat in sugar and whip until stiff. In another bowl, mix flour, salt, and coconut together. Fold this mixture into egg whites. Drop by heaping tablespoonfuls onto a greased and floured cookie sheet. Bake in a preheated 300° oven for 18 to 20 minutes or until slightly golden. Allow cookies to cool on the baking sheet. Makes 4 dozen.

How to Make a Chalkboard Sign

Materials

- ✦ old picture frame—choose one with unique character and a sturdy backboard (if no backboard, use a thin piece of laminated plywood cut to size)
- ✦ paint for frame
- ✦ gray primer (spray or bottle)
- ✦ basic black chalkboard paint (spray or bottle)
- ✦ paint brush and drop cloth

1. Remove the frame's glass and backboard.
2. Clean and paint the frame. Set aside to fully dry.
3. Apply multiple light coats of primer to backboard. Allow to dry 24 hours.
4. Apply multiple light coats of chalkboard paint to backboard. If using a brush, sand the board with fine grit sandpaper between coats to smooth out brush lines. Allow to dry for 24 hours.
5. Replace the backboard into the frame and display.

As gold more splendid from the fire appears;
Thus friendship brightens by the length of years.

THOMAS CARLYLE

Hark, hark! I hear
The strain of strutting chanticleer
Cry, cock-a-diddle-dow.

WILLIAM SHAKESPEARE

LIFE IS TO BE FORTIFIED BY MANY FRIENDSHIPS. TO LOVE
AND TO BE LOVED IS THE GREATEST HAPPINESS OF EXISTENCE.

SYDNEY SMITH

Yes'm, old friends is
always best, 'less you can
catch a new one that's fit
to make an old one out of.

SARAH ORNE JEWETT

The best friend is he that,
when he wishes a person's
good, wishes it for that
person's own sake.

ARISTOTLE

HAPPINESS RESIDES
NOT IN POSSESSIONS
AND NOT IN GOLD; THE
FEELING OF HAPPINESS
DWELLS IN THE SOUL.

DEMOCRITUS

*Walk with
the wise and
become wise.*

THE BOOK OF PROVERBS

Poppycock

1 (10-ounce) bag of popcorn (popped)
1 cup butter
2 cups brown sugar
½ cup white corn syrup
1 teaspoon salt
1 teaspoon butter flavoring extract
½ teaspoon baking soda
almonds, peanuts, or other nuts of choice

In a large saucepan, melt the butter. Add the brown sugar and corn syrup and cook for 5 minutes, stirring occasionally. Remove from heat and add butter flavoring extract and baking soda. Stir in nuts. In a very large bowl, pour caramel syrup over the popcorn. Stir quickly. Pour the mixture onto cookie sheets and bake at 250° for 1 hour, turning mixture after 30 minutes. Cool slightly, break apart, and when cooled completely, store in airtight containers.

THANK YOU FOR BEING MY FRIEND.

Post Card